GOODMAN'S FIVE-STAR
ACTIVITY BOOKS

Test-Taker Practice Series

LEVEL D

Burton Goodman

JAMESTOWN PUBLISHERS

a division of NTC/CONTEMPORARY PUBLISHING GROUP
Lincolnwood, Illinois USA

Acknowledgments

Stories, articles, adaptations, and other instructional materials by Burton Goodman.

The author wishes to express profound gratitude to Matthew Goodman for his invaluable assistance.

Cover Design
    Karen Christoffersen
Interior Illustrations
    Other Brother Design

ISBN: 0-8092-0448-7
Published by Jamestown Publishers,
a division of NTC/Contemporary Publishing Group, Inc.,
4255 West Touhy Avenue,
Lincolnwood (Chicago), Illinois, 60712-1975, U.S.A.

CONTENTS

ABOUT THE SERIES

Goodman's Five-Star Activity Book, Level D reinforces and extends the exercises and literary themes in *Surprises* and *More Surprises* in *Goodman's Five-Star Stories,* Level D. This activity book can be used in conjunction with *Surprises* and *More Surprises,* or it can be used on a completely independent basis.

Goodman's Five-Star Activity Books
Test-Taker Practice Series

The *Goodman's Five-Star Activity Books* series has been specially designed to help students master the kinds of exercises most frequently found on standardized tests. The series uses high-quality multicultural nonfiction and fiction materials to familiarize students with the kinds of questions they are likely to encounter. At the same time, the books offer students numerous opportunities to improve their language arts skills and their test scores through practice.

Each book in the series focuses on developing skills and competencies in reading comprehension, mechanics, and writing. Provision is also made for study skills practice.

The **Reading Comprehension** section provides students with 10 standardized questions with an emphasis on critical thinking and vocabulary. The **Mechanics** section offers repeated practice in capitalization, punctuation, the comma, spelling, and grammar. The **Writing** section requires students to respond to a wide variety of specific and open-ended writing tasks.

The series includes a practical Test-Taker self-scoring feature that enables students to score and record their results.

Used along with the books in *Goodman's Five-Star Stories*, or on an independent basis, I feel certain that the *Goodman's Five-Star Activity Books* will help students develop the confidence and competency to improve their test scores. In addition, the books will help readers master many of the essential language arts skills they need for success in school and in life.

Burton Goodman

The Mouse

based on a story by Saki

Theodore Voler's mother had always tried to
protect him from what she called "the
unpleasant things in life." She did this from
the time he was a child until he was a
grown man. During those years she let
nothing bother or upset her dear Theodore.
So after she died, Theodore found himself
living in a world that was not as nice as he
thought it should be.

For Theodore, even a simple train ride
was filled with problems. One September morning he made his
way to his compartment[1] on the train. As he sat down, he felt
nervous and annoyed.

He had been staying at the country house of a friend and his
family. They were very pleasant to Theodore. Of course, the
house was not neat enough to suit him. It was also very poorly
run. Nobody seemed to know what jobs to do.

For example, the family knew that Theodore was supposed
to return home today. But nobody remembered to send for the
horse and carriage to take Theodore to the station. At the last
minute, Theodore had to harness a horse himself. This meant he
had to move about in a dark, damp stable. The place smelled of
horses, and he thought he saw mice. The whole thing made him
feel a little bit sick.

1. compartment: a very small room with seats on a train.

For additional exercises and another story by Saki, which also ends with a
surprise, see "Mrs. Packletide's Tiger" in *More Surprises* in *Goodman's Five-Star
Stories,* Level D.

As the train left the station, Theodore imagined that he still smelled like the stable. He was afraid there might even be a few pieces of straw somewhere on his neat clothing. Luckily, the only other person in the car was a woman about his own age—and she was fast asleep.

The train was speeding along. Suddenly Theodore was horrified to discover that he was not alone in the car with the sleeping woman. In fact, he was not even alone in his own clothes! He felt a warm, creeping movement over his skin. Theodore knew immediately that it was a mouse. It must have crawled up his pants leg when he was in the stable.

Theodore stamped his feet. He shook his legs wildly. No matter what he did, he could not get rid of the mouse. Theodore sat back and thought about what to do. The train would not stop for another hour, but it was not possible for him to go on like this for 60 more minutes.

He knew the only way to get rid of the mouse was to take off his clothes. But how could he undress in front of a woman? The idea made him turn red. It filled him with shame.

Yet the woman was sound asleep. The mouse, on the other hand, was not. He could feel it moving under his clothing.

Theodore finally decided to take action. He quickly and quietly tied a blanket to the racks that were on both sides of the compartment. This made a little dressing room that hid him from the sleeping woman.

He hurriedly removed pieces of clothing until the mouse finally appeared. It suddenly jumped onto the floor. As it did, the blanket fell down. Just then the sleeping woman woke up!

Theodore moved almost as quickly as the mouse. He grabbed the blanket and threw it around his half-dressed body. Then he fell back into his seat.

Theodore's heart was beating wildly. What would the woman think? What would the woman do? Would she call for the conductor and have him taken away? Yet all she did was gaze very calmly at him.

Theodore wondered what he could say that would explain why he was covered by a blanket. Finally he said, "I . . . I think I caught a chill."

"I am sorry to hear that," was all she replied.

Theodore wondered if he could tell her the truth. So he asked, "Are you afraid of mice?"

"Not really," she answered. "But why do you ask?"

"There was one crawling inside my clothes just now. I had to get rid of it while you were asleep. That's what . . . that's what . . . brought me to this."

The woman seemed surprised. She said, "How did getting rid of a mouse bring on a chill?"

Theodore wondered, "Is she making fun of me?" Suddenly Theodore became terrified. He realized that the train was moving closer and closer to the next station. The train would be there before very long! Then dozens of eyes, not just hers, would see him this way. He was still half-dressed and covered by a blanket!

He had only one hope now. The woman might fall asleep again. But as the minutes ticked by, that last hope began to fade. Then the woman said, "We must be close to the station now."

Her words moved him to action. Like a hunted animal making a mad dash to safety, Theodore dropped the blanket. He struggled to get back into his clothes. He did not dare to look at the silent woman near him. His head was pounding, and he felt as if he were choking. He thought he would go out of his mind.

Finally Theodore managed to get back into his clothes. He sank back into his seat, at last. He was worn out and exhausted.

The train began to slow down. Then the woman spoke. She said, "Would you be kind enough to find me a taxi when we get to the station? I hate to trouble you when you're not feeling well. But since I'm blind, I always need a bit of help at a railroad station."

Go on ➤

I. Reading Comprehension Skills

Fill in the circle next to the correct answer.

1. What is this story mostly about?
   - (A) an unusual event on a train
   - (B) the problems that come up when you visit a family
   - (C) how to get rid of mice
   - (D) a woman who falls asleep

2. Which words belong in Box 1?
   - (A) often did bold things
   - (B) discovered that the world was not as nice as he wished
   - (C) did not care if people were careless
   - (D) never got nervous

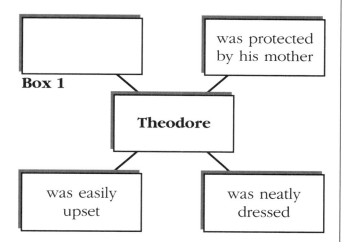

Box 1

was protected by his mother

Theodore

was easily upset

was neatly dressed

3. To get to the station, Theodore had to
   - (A) take a taxi.
   - (B) walk all the way.
   - (C) ask someone to drive him.
   - (D) harness a horse.

4. Theodore finally got rid of the mouse by
   - (A) jumping up and down.
   - (B) shouting at it.
   - (C) taking off some clothes.
   - (D) stamping his feet.

5. Which statement is *not* true?
   - (A) Theodore discovered that there was a mouse under his clothes.
   - (B) The woman on the train was not afraid of mice.
   - (C) Theodore's actions made the woman angry.
   - (D) Theodore covered himself with a blanket.

Answers

1. (A) (B) (C) (D)
2. (A) (B) (C) (D)
3. (A) (B) (C) (D)
4. (A) (B) (C) (D)
5. (A) (B) (C) (D)

Go on ➤

6. Theodore did not have to worry about the woman on the train because she
   - (A) was willing to help him.
   - (B) was too frightened to do anything.
   - (C) liked him very much.
   - (D) could not see.

7. The main purpose of the story is to
   - (A) give the reader facts.
   - (B) amuse the reader.
   - (C) make the reader feel sad.
   - (D) scare the reader.

8. Theodore was feeling nervous and annoyed. The word *annoyed* means
   - (A) bothered.
   - (B) pleased.
   - (C) foolish.
   - (D) worried.

9. The idea made him turn red and filled him with shame. When you feel *shame*, you think that you have done
   - A something wrong.
   - B something well.
   - C something unusual.
   - D your best.

10. Theodore became terrified when he realized that the train was coming into the station. The word *terrified* means
    - (A) filled with joy.
    - (B) filled with fear.
    - (C) pleasantly surprised.
    - (D) very hungry.

Answers

6.	(A)	(B)	(C)	(D)
7.	(A)	(B)	(C)	(D)
8.	(A)	(B)	(C)	(D)
9.	(A)	(B)	(C)	(D)
10.	(A)	(B)	(C)	(D)

How many questions did you answer correctly? Circle your score below. Then fill in your **Comprehension** score on the **Test-Taker Score Chart** on the inside of the back cover.

Number Correct	1	2	3	4	5	6	7	8	9	10
My Score	10	20	30	40	50	60	70	80	90	100

Go on ➤

II. Mechanics (capitalization, punctuation, the comma, spelling, and grammar)

Fill in the circle next to the correct answer.

1. Which sentence has a mistake in capitalization?
   - Ⓐ The name of this story is "The Mouse."
   - Ⓑ It takes place somewhere in England.
   - Ⓒ Theodore got on a train one September morning.
   - Ⓓ at last Theodore sank back into his seat.

2. Which sentence is not punctuated correctly?
   - Ⓐ The train was speeding along.
   - Ⓑ I hate to trouble you when you're not feeling well.
   - Ⓒ Theodore exclaimed, "I must do something at once!"
   - Ⓓ Were you surprised by the ending of the story.

3. Which sentence needs a comma or does not use the comma correctly?
   - Ⓐ The stable was cold damp, and dark.
   - Ⓑ He hoped that she would fall asleep, but she did not.
   - Ⓒ Theodore was tired, nervous, and upset.
   - Ⓓ The train slowed down and stopped.

4. Which sentence has a mistake in spelling in the **underlined** word?
   - Ⓐ Theodore was <u>afraid</u> that he had straw on his clothes.
   - Ⓑ After a while, the mouse <u>finally</u> appeared.
   - Ⓒ He was <u>useing</u> a blanket to cover himself.
   - Ⓓ Theodore did not visit his friend <u>again</u>.

5. Which sentence has a mistake in grammar?
   - Ⓐ The people at the country house were pleasant to him.
   - Ⓑ Theodore thought he seen mice in the stable.
   - Ⓒ He began to tie a blanket to the racks.
   - Ⓓ His head was pounding.

Answers
1. Ⓐ Ⓑ Ⓒ Ⓓ
2. Ⓐ Ⓑ Ⓒ Ⓓ
3. Ⓐ Ⓑ Ⓒ Ⓓ
4. Ⓐ Ⓑ Ⓒ Ⓓ
5. Ⓐ Ⓑ Ⓒ Ⓓ

How many questions did you answer correctly? Circle your score below. Then fill in your **Mechanics** score on the **Test-Taker Score Chart** on the inside of the back cover.

Number Correct	1	2	3	4	5
Your Score	20	40	60	80	100

Go on ➤

III. Writing

Answer the questions. You may look back at the story as often as you wish.

1. Use the chart to put the events in the order in which they happened. Write the correct letter in each box. Two letters have been done for you.

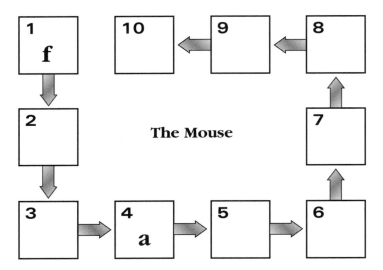

a. Theodore tied a blanket to the racks.

b. The mouse leaped to the floor, and the blanket fell down.

c. Theodore sat down in the compartment.

d. The sleeping woman woke up.

e. Theodore got back into his clothes.

f. Theodore made his way to his compartment on the train.

g. The woman asked Theodore to find a taxi for her.

h. Theodore removed some pieces of clothing.

i. Theodore discovered that there was a mouse under his clothes.

j. Theodore grabbed the blanket and threw it around his body.

Go on ▶

2. Suppose that the woman on the train had been able to see. How do you think the story would have ended?

_____

_____

_____

_____

_____

3. Pretend that you are Theodore. Make believe you are telling a friend about your train ride home. On the lines below, write what you would say.

   It all started when I_____

_____

_____

_____

_____

_____

_____

_____

_____

_____

_____

_____

_____

_____

_____

Stop

Josh Gibson and the Quick Home Run

It has been many years since Josh Gibson last played in a
baseball game. Fans who saw him play say that no one could
hit a baseball harder or farther than Josh Gibson could. People
still tell stories about Gibson the Great. Sometimes it is hard to
tell where the truth ends and the legend begins.

The following story certainly is not true. Still, it will give
you an idea of the awe[1] felt by those who watched Josh
Gibson play.

According to the tale, Gibson's team was playing one day
in Pittsburgh, Pennsylvania. Gibson was at bat. He hit a ball
that just seemed to keep rising in the sky. Everyone in the
park looked up. They waited for the ball to come down—but
it never did. Five minutes later the umpires finally decided to
give Gibson a home run.

The story doesn't end there. The next day Gibson's team
was playing in Philadelphia—more than 250 miles away. A
baseball suddenly fell from the sky. The center fielder reached
out and caught it.

1. awe: a feeling of great respect and wonder.

For additional exercises and more stories about baseball, see "The Southpaw" in
Surprises and "One Throw" in *More Surprises* in *Goodman's Five-Star Stories,* Level D.

The umpire hurried over to Gibson. "You're out!" he exclaimed, pointing at Josh. "Yesterday, in Pittsburgh!"

Of course, this never really happened. But the story demonstrates how people felt about Josh Gibson.

Here is a story that really *did* take place. Once in a game in Indianapolis, the pitcher threw a very slow pitch to Gibson. Gibson began to swing too early, and his left hand flew off the bat. Somehow Gibson was able to hit the ball—and soon it was soaring high over the outfield fence. The pitcher shook his head as Gibson trotted around the bases. Gibson was so strong that he had hit a home run holding the bat with only one hand!

Gibson's home runs were called "quick" home runs. This is because they traveled so quickly that they seemed to go out of the park before the outfielders had enough time to turn around.

For example, there was the home run Gibson hit in a game played in San Juan, Puerto Rico. The ball went over the fence. It sailed across the street. Finally, it flew over the wall of a prison across from the ballpark. The ball landed near a surprised group of prisoners in the prison yard.

The great home run hitter Babe Ruth once hit a ball that went 550 feet. That was Ruth's longest home run. But *many* of Josh Gibson's home runs went more than 500 feet. One home run at Wrigley Field in Chicago might have gone 700 feet if it had not hit the scoreboard clock.

Gibson played baseball from 1930 to 1946. During that time he hit more than 1,000 home runs. He was one of the greatest home run hitters of his time—in fact, of *all* time. But Josh Gibson never played in the major leagues.

Gibson never played there because he was an African American, and the unwritten rule of his time prevented African Americans from playing in the major leagues. Gibson spent his years playing for teams such as the Homestead Grays, in what were known as the Negro Leagues.

Gibson was one of the most famous stars of the Negro Leagues. In 1943 he was paid $1,500 a month—a huge amount of money then—to play for the Pittsburgh Crawfords. How well did Gibson do? He led the league in hitting with a .526 average. This means that he got a hit more than half the times he came to bat!

On January 20, 1947, Gibson suddenly got sick, and he died soon after. He was only 35 years old. Just a few months later, Jackie Robinson joined the Brooklyn Dodgers. He was the first African American to challenge major league baseball's "color line." Once Jackie Robinson began playing in the major leagues, baseball changed forever. Today, anyone who has enough talent can play in the major leagues.

Josh Gibson was good enough, but he never got the chance to prove it. Still, he is considered one of the greatest baseball players of all time. In 1972—25 years after his death—Gibson was elected to baseball's Hall of Fame. It is the highest honor any baseball player can receive. If you go to the Hall of Fame in Cooperstown, New York, you can see a uniform that Gibson wore when he played baseball.

Yes, Josh Gibson is remembered in baseball's Hall of Fame. But he is remembered in other ways too. He will probably live on in the stories people tell—tales about Gibson the Great, the man who hit 1,000 of the quickest home runs ever seen.

I. Reading Comprehension Skills

Fill in the circle next to the correct answer.

1. What is this article mostly about?
   - Ⓐ a funny thing that happened in a baseball game
   - Ⓑ how to play baseball
   - Ⓒ Josh Gibson, a great home run hitter
   - Ⓓ people who have played baseball throughout the years

2. Gibson's home runs were called "quick" because they
   - Ⓐ went out of the park so fast.
   - Ⓑ went very high.
   - Ⓒ took a long time to come down.
   - Ⓓ sometimes went very far.

3. Gibson played baseball from
   - Ⓐ 1920 to 1930.
   - Ⓑ 1930 to 1946.
   - Ⓒ 1946 to 1960.
   - Ⓓ 1960 to 1970.

4. Which statement is *not* true?
   - Ⓐ Gibson made $1,500 a month in 1943.
   - Ⓑ Some of Gibson's home runs went more than 500 feet.
   - Ⓒ Gibson played for the Brooklyn Dodgers.
   - Ⓓ Gibson was elected to baseball's Hall of Fame.

5. What was true of Jackie Robinson?
   - Ⓐ He never played in the major leagues.
   - Ⓑ He died in 1947.
   - Ⓒ He played in the Negro Leagues until he died.
   - Ⓓ He led the way for other African-American players to play in the major leagues.

6. The writer thinks that Josh Gibson
   - Ⓐ was not as good as most of today's baseball players.
   - Ⓑ once hit a ball that traveled more than 250 miles.
   - Ⓒ was one of the best baseball players of all time.
   - Ⓓ was not very strong.

Answers

1. Ⓐ Ⓑ Ⓒ Ⓓ
2. Ⓐ Ⓑ Ⓒ Ⓓ
3. Ⓐ Ⓑ Ⓒ Ⓓ
4. Ⓐ Ⓑ Ⓒ Ⓓ
5. Ⓐ Ⓑ Ⓒ Ⓓ
6. Ⓐ Ⓑ Ⓒ Ⓓ

Go on ➤

7. The article suggests that if Gibson had played in the major leagues, he would

Ⓐ not have done very well.

Ⓑ have become a star.

Ⓒ have hit 5,000 home runs.

Ⓓ not have gotten into the Hall of Fame.

8. This article demonstrates how far Gibson could hit a baseball. The word *demonstrates* means

Ⓐ shows.

Ⓑ asks.

Ⓒ likes.

Ⓓ wonders.

9. At one time African-American players were prevented from playing in the major leagues. The word *prevented* means

Ⓐ paid.

Ⓑ noticed.

Ⓒ stopped.

Ⓓ helped.

10. Today, anyone who has enough talent can play in the major leagues. If you have *talent*, this means that you

Ⓐ have money.

Ⓑ have many friends.

Ⓒ enjoy sports.

Ⓓ do something very well.

Answers

7.	Ⓐ	Ⓑ	Ⓒ	Ⓓ
8.	Ⓐ	Ⓑ	Ⓒ	Ⓓ
9.	Ⓐ	Ⓑ	Ⓒ	Ⓓ
10.	Ⓐ	Ⓑ	Ⓒ	Ⓓ

How many questions did you answer correctly? Circle your score below. Then fill in your **Comprehension** score on the **Test-Taker Score Chart** on the inside of the back cover.

Number Correct	1	2	3	4	5	6	7	8	9	10
My Score	10	20	30	40	50	60	70	80	90	100

Go on ➤

II. Mechanics (capitalization, punctuation, the comma, spelling and grammar)

Fill in the circle next to the correct answer.

1. Which sentence has a mistake in capitalization?
   - (A) Josh Gibson hit a long home run in Wrigley Field in Chicago.
   - (B) Some of his home runs broke seats in the park.
   - (C) Jackie Robinson played for the Brooklyn Dodgers.
   - (D) Gibson's team was called the pittsburgh Crawfords.

2. Which sentence has a mistake in punctuation?
   - (A) One of Babe Ruth's home runs went 550 feet.
   - (B) The pitcher couldn't believe what happened.
   - (C) Gibson wasnt allowed to play in the major leagues.
   - (D) How many home runs did Gibson hit?

3. Which sentence needs a comma or does not use the comma correctly?
   - (A) Gibson hit a long home run in San Juan Puerto Rico.
   - (B) Gibson, Ruth, and Robinson are in baseball's Hall of Fame.
   - (C) Ruth, a great home run hitter, played for the New York Yankees.
   - (D) Gibson died on January 20, 1947.

4. Which sentence has a mistake in spelling in the **underlined** word?
   - (A) It is the highest honor anyone can <u>receive</u>.
   - (B) The pitcher <u>threw</u> Gibson a very slow pitch.
   - (C) The ball went over the fence and landed <u>accross</u> the street.
   - (D) Some of the stories about Gibson are very <u>amusing</u>.

5. Which sentence has a mistake in grammar?
   - (A) Jackie Robinson was a very fast runner.
   - (B) Gibson and Ruth has hit many home runs.
   - (C) My grandfather saw Ruth play.
   - (D) Many stories about Gibson are true.

Answers

1. (A) (B) (C) (D)
2. (A) (B) (C) (D)
3. (A) (B) (C) (D)
4. (A) (B) (C) (D)
5. (A) (B) (C) (D)

How many questions did you answer correctly? Circle your score below. Then fill in your **Mechanics** score on the **Test-Taker Score Chart** on the inside of the back cover.

Number Correct	1	2	3	4	5
Your Score	20	40	60	80	100

Go on ➤

III. Writing

Answer the questions. You may look back at the story as often as you wish.

1. In each circle in the graphic organizer below, write one fact about Josh Gibson.

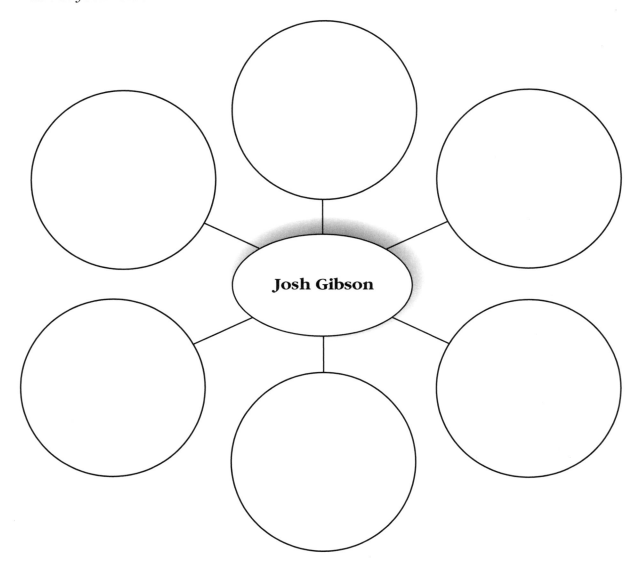

2. Read the following statement:

   Josh Gibson was one of the greatest home run hitters who ever lived.

   Use facts and examples from the article to prove that this statement is true. Look at the graphic organizer you filled in for question 1 to help you write your answer.

   _____

   _____

   _____

   _____

   _____

   _____

   _____

   _____

3. Think about a sport or a game that you enjoy. Then tell what you like about the one that you chose.

   _____

   _____

   _____

   _____

   _____

   _____

   _____

   _____

Go on ➤

IV. Study Skills

Reading a Table. Study the table below. Then answer the questions that follow. Use complete sentences.

Jackie Robinson's
First Five Years in the Major Leagues

YEAR	GAMES	BATTING AVERAGE	HITS	HOME RUNS	RUNS BATTED IN
1947	151	.297	175	12	48
1948	147	.296	170	12	85
1949	156	.342	203	16	124
1950	144	.328	170	14	81
1951	153	.338	185	19	88

1. How many games did Jackie Robinson play in 1947?

   _____

2. How many home runs did Robinson hit in 1948?

   _____

3. In what year did Robinson have a batting average of .342?

   _____

4. How many hits did Robinson get in 1950?

   _____

Go on ➤

5. In what year did Robinson have the most runs batted in?

_____

6. In what year did Robinson have the most home runs?

_____

7. In what year did Robinson get the most hits?'

_____

8. How many games did Robinson play in 1951?

_____

9. In what year did Robinson play in the fewest games?

_____

10. What was Robinson's batting average in 1951?

_____

A Gift for the General

General Chen lived in a city in China a long time ago. He was a great general whose well-trained army always defeated the country's enemies.

Everyone treated the general with respect. Now and then he received gifts from people he knew as well as from strangers. General Chen was often heard to say, "It is better to give than to receive." Then he always smiled and added, "But I like to receive."

Perhaps that is the reason he got so many gifts. People probably thought that there were worse things in life than being on the good side of a powerful general.

One day the general received a gift that was truly amazing. It was a huge elephant. The elephant stood as high as it was long, and it stood very high.

An elephant in China was a rare sight in those days. And an elephant of that size—well, you can imagine how General Chen's servants stared at the beast in the courtyard.

"What a magnificent elephant!" the general exclaimed. "I must show it to my friends."

So the general arranged for his friends to come to a party at his home. Famous and important people hurried to the general's mansion. You see, word of the enormous elephant had spread throughout the city. Everyone was curious to look at the beast.

For additional exercises and another story about gifts, see "The Gift of the Magi"
in *Surprises* in *Goodman's Five-Star Stories*, Level D.

Among the guests were many well-known people. They had the best and the brightest minds in the city. There were scientists and artists. There were also important men who, like the general, were in the army.

When the general judged that the time was right, he led everyone to the courtyard. There one and all gazed with wonder and delight at the general's elephant.

"What an astonishing elephant!" the guests said to one other. They shook the general's hand, while the general beamed with pleasure.

Then someone said, "Tell us, general. How much does the elephant weigh?"

The general turned to his chief aide.[1] "Tell me," said the general, "how much does this elephant weigh?"

The aide thought for a moment. Then he answered. "Why it weighs very much."

"Yes," said the general, "but *how much* does it weigh?"

"That is not possible to know," said the aide. "You see," he explained, "we do not have a scale big enough to weigh an elephant. So no one can say what this elephant weighs."

The general turned to his guests. As I have said, his guests had the best and the brightest minds in the city.

"Surely," said the general, "there must be *some* way to find out what this elephant weighs. Can anyone think of a way?"

The guests were silent until the aide spoke up. "You see, general," he explained once again, "there is no scale big enough for an elephant, so it is impossible to know how much this elephant weighs."

"Yes," the guests murmured to each other, as they nodded their heads, "it is impossible to know how much this elephant weighs."

1. **aide:** helper.

General Chen's little daughter had been listening with interest to this. "Excuse me, father," she said, "but I think I know how to find out how much the elephant weighs."

General Chen smiled. "Dear daughter," he said, "do you believe that you can succeed when my guests here could not?"

"It is easy," said the child. "You must lead the elephant onto a boat by the dock at the edge of the river. The weight of the elephant will push the boat down into the water. The water will make a water line around the boat."

"Yes?" said the father.

"Then lead the elephant back to the shore. When the elephant is off the boat, the boat will rise in the water. Fill the boat with stones until it sinks to the same water line around the boat. Weigh all of the stones. The weight of the stones is the elephant's weight."

General Chen snapped his fingers and servants came forward.

General Chen commanded, "Lead the elephant onto a boat by the dock at the edge of the river!"

That is what they did. They led the elephant onto the boat, and later they led it away. They filled the boat with stones until it sank to the same level it was at under the elephant's weight. Then they weighed the stones and found out how much the elephant weighed.

General Chen was delighted. Once again, he invited his friends to a party at his house.

After everyone arrived, the general said, "I have made this party in honor of my daughter. I think you must agree that she is a genius[2]."

One of the guests frowned. "A genius!" he said. "Why, her plan was not very hard. In fact, it was easy. Anyone here might have thought of that plan."

"Ah, yes," said General Chen, "but nobody did. It seems simple enough *now*—now that it has been done. But it took a genius to think of it first!"

Who could say that was not so? Nobody could. And there was no prouder man in all of China than General Chen.

2. **genius:** someone who has a great mind.

Go on ➤

I. Reading Comprehension Skills

Fill in the circle next to the correct answer.

1. What is the main idea of this story?
   - Ⓐ It is not possible to weigh an elephant.
   - Ⓑ It is better to give than to receive.
   - Ⓒ A young girl explains how to weigh an elephant.
   - Ⓓ Elephants were rare in China long ago.

2. People wanted to be "on the good side" of General Chen. This means that people
   - Ⓐ wanted to stand right behind the general.
   - Ⓑ wanted General Chen to like them.
   - Ⓒ wanted to be where General Chen could see them.
   - Ⓓ didn't know if General Chen was on their side.

3. The general's guests were very smart, but they
   - Ⓐ were not famous.
   - Ⓑ did not like General Chen.
   - Ⓒ could not figure out how to weigh an elephant.
   - Ⓓ were not artists or scientists.

4. Which sentence is *not* true?
   - Ⓐ The story took place a long time ago.
   - Ⓑ People were curious to see the elephant.
   - Ⓒ The daughter's plan worked.
   - Ⓓ General Chen did not like to get gifts.

5. If the stones weighed 4,000 pounds, how much did the elephant weigh?
   - Ⓐ about 3,500 pounds
   - Ⓑ a little more than 4,000 pounds
   - Ⓒ much less than 4,000 pounds
   - Ⓓ 4,000 pounds

6. How did the general feel at the end of the story?
   - Ⓐ very pleased
   - Ⓑ very sad
   - Ⓒ very angry
   - Ⓓ very worried

Answers			
1. Ⓐ	Ⓑ	Ⓒ	Ⓓ
2. Ⓐ	Ⓑ	Ⓒ	Ⓓ
3. Ⓐ	Ⓑ	Ⓒ	Ⓓ
4. Ⓐ	Ⓑ	Ⓒ	Ⓓ
5. Ⓐ	Ⓑ	Ⓒ	Ⓓ
6. Ⓐ	Ⓑ	Ⓒ	Ⓓ

Go on ➤

7. The story suggests that
   - (A) young people do not know as much as they think they do.
   - (B) guests can sometimes be helpful.
   - (C) most scales are too small to use.
   - (D) it seems easy to figure out a problem after it has been solved.

8. The general's well-trained army always defeated the enemy. The word *defeated* means
   - (A) met.
   - (B) beat.
   - (C) ran away from.
   - (D) lost to.

9. "What a magnificent elephant!" exclaimed the general. The word *magnificent* means
   - (A) happy or cheerful.
   - (B) little or small.
   - (C) great or grand.
   - (D) fast or quick.

10. They went to a party at the general's mansion. A *mansion* is
    - (A) a large house.
    - (B) an office.
    - (C) a store.
    - (D) a garden.

Answers

7.	(A)	(B)	(C)	(D)
8.	(A)	(B)	(C)	(D)
9.	(A)	(B)	(C)	(D)
10.	(A)	(B)	(C)	(D)

How many questions did you answer correctly? Circle your score below. Then fill in your **Comprehension** score on the **Test-Taker Score Chart** on the inside of the back cover.

Number Correct	1	2	3	4	5	6	7	8	9	10
My Score	10	20	30	40	50	60	70	80	90	100

Go on ➤

II. Mechanics (capitalization, punctuation, the comma, spelling, and grammar)

Fill in the circle next to the correct answer.

1. Which sentence has a mistake in capitalization?
   - Ⓐ Everyone treated General Chen with respect.
   - Ⓑ The story takes place in a city in china.
   - Ⓒ One of the general's friends was Dr. Lee.
   - Ⓓ You know that I like to get gifts.

2. Which sentence is not punctuated correctly?
   - Ⓐ Many people came to the generals house.
   - Ⓑ They didn't know how much the elephant weighed.
   - Ⓒ A guest exclaimed, "What an amazing elephant!"
   - Ⓓ His daughter knew how to figure out the elephant's weight.

3. Which sentence needs a comma or does not use the comma correctly?
   - Ⓐ The elephant was tall, wide, and heavy.
   - Ⓑ Word of the elephant spread throughout the city, and everyone wanted to see the beast.
   - Ⓒ Yes, it was an enormous animal.
   - Ⓓ The guests were smart but they were not able to solve the problem.

4. Which sentence has a mistake in spelling in the underlined word?
   - Ⓐ It was the <u>biggest</u> beast they had ever seen.
   - Ⓑ The elephant swung <u>its</u> trunk from side to side.
   - Ⓒ He received gifts from people he knew and from strangers <u>to</u>.
   - Ⓓ The general waited <u>until</u> all the guests arrived.

5. Which one has a mistake in grammar?
   - Ⓐ All of the guests were famous.
   - Ⓑ He thought that his daughter was a genius.
   - Ⓒ The servants took the elephant to the dock.
   - Ⓓ Take the stones off the boat weigh the stones later.

Answers

1. Ⓐ Ⓑ Ⓒ Ⓓ
2. Ⓐ Ⓑ Ⓒ Ⓓ
3. Ⓐ Ⓑ Ⓒ Ⓓ
4. Ⓐ Ⓑ Ⓒ Ⓓ
5. Ⓐ Ⓑ Ⓒ Ⓓ

How many questions did you answer correctly? Circle your score below. Then fill in your **Mechanics** score on the **Test-Taker Score Chart** on the inside of the back cover.

Number Correct	1	2	3	4	5
Your Score	20	40	60	80	100

Go on ➤

III. Writing

Answer the questions. You may look back at the story as often as you wish.

1. General Chen invited guests to two parties. At the first party, General Chen showed off his elephant. At the second party, he honored his daughter. Which party do you think the general enjoyed more? Explain your answer.

_____

_____

_____

_____

_____

_____

2. General Chen stated that his daughter was a genius. Do you agree with him? Give reasons and examples to support your answer.

I thought that General Chen's daughter _____

_____

_____

_____

_____

_____

_____

_____

_____

Go on ➤

3. In "A Gift for the General," General Chen's daughter explained how to weigh an elephant. Write about a time when someone taught you how to do something or when you taught someone else.

Give as many facts as you can. Be sure to include the following:

- what was taught

- who did the teaching

- where and when it happened

Be sure to check your writing for correct spelling, capitalization, punctuation, and grammar.

_____

_____

_____

_____

_____

_____

_____

_____

_____

_____

_____

_____

_____

_____

_____

_____

_____

Stop

The First Cowboys

You probably have seen many cowboys—in
pictures or in real life. It is easy to recognize
cowboys, even when they're not riding horses.
You'll know them by their high leather boots
and big ten-gallon hats. Do you know where
that name comes from? The hat is so large that
people said it could hold 10 gallons of water.

Cowboys must do many different jobs. Perhaps a cowboy's
most important jobs are herding cattle and protecting them
from wild animals and cattle robbers. This often means
working from morning to sundown in cold or rainy weather.
Therefore, it is not surprising that cowboys must have strength,
endurance, and courage.

Maybe that is why the cowboy has come to represent
values that many Americans admire. Two of these values are
working hard and being independent. In fact, to many people
the cowboy represents, or is a symbol of, honor. After all, just
look at how many movies have cowboys as heroes.

Many of those movies show cowboys fighting with Native
American Indians in the Old West. But did you know that the
first cowboys were actually Native American Indians? You may
find this hard to believe, but it's true.

For additional exercises and more stories about cowboys, see "Gold-Mounted
Guns" in *Surprises* and "Little Stranger" in *More Surprises* in *Goodman's Five-Star
Stories,* Level D.

Spanish explorers settled in Mexico in the early 1500s. They brought with them sheep, cattle, and horses—animals that had never been seen in North America before.

The Spanish settlers built huge ranches where they kept their cattle. Some of the ranches had as many as 150,000 cattle. Who would take care of all these cattle? The settlers did not want to do all the work themselves. So they trained many Mexican Indians to work on the cattle ranches. The Mexican cattle workers became known as *vaqueros* (vah KER ohs) from the Spanish word *vaca*, which means "cow."

The *vaqueros* were the first cowboys. They quickly learned how to ride horses. Soon they were among the best riders in the world. They were proud horsemen. It was said that a *vaquero* would never walk if he could ride. In fact, a true *vaquero* took pride in being bowlegged. This means having legs that were curved from many hours of riding a horse.

Vaqueros had to know much more than just how to ride a horse. A *vaquero* also had to be an expert with a long rope, which in Spanish is called a *reata* (ree AH tuh). Some *reatas* were 100 feet long. *Vaqueros* used the ropes to catch and tie up cattle. A skilled *vaquero* could catch a running animal that was nearly 75 feet away. One time, a *vaquero* even used his *reata* to catch a low-flying eagle.

A *vaquero* lived a very hard life. His house was just a small wooden hut or shack. His bed was a straw mat on the ground. For meals, he usually ate simple corn tortillas. A *vaquero's* shirt and pants were made of plain cotton.

Vaqueros wore big, wide hats to protect themselves from the sun, wind, and rain. These hats are called sombreros, which comes from the Spanish word *sombra*, meaning "shade." The first *vaqueros* did not wear leather boots. In fact, the very first *vaqueros* did not wear shoes at all.

In 1848, following the war between the United States and Mexico, the United States gained a very large piece of Mexico's land. This territory later became California, Nevada, Utah, and parts of some other western states.

The *vaqueros* had been working with cattle on that land for nearly 300 years. Now they showed the new American settlers how to be cowboys. They taught the Americans how to rope cattle. They showed them how to keep the cattle together in large herds and how to drive them great distances.

The new American cowboys learned many things from the *vaqueros*. The Americans got something else too—many new words for their language. For example, another word for cowboy is *buckaroo*. Do you know where that word comes from? Instead of saying "vah KER oh," Americans said "bak HAR oh." After many years, the word became *buckaroo*. A cowboy's rope is called a lariat. That comes from *la reata,* meaning "the rope."

To this day, many of the cowboys of the American West are Mexican American. They are the proud descendants of the Mexican *vaqueros*—the Mexican Indians who were the first cowboys.

Go on ➤

I. Reading Comprehension Skills

Fill in the circle next to the correct answer.

1. This article is mostly about
   Ⓐ how to herd cattle.
   Ⓑ the earliest cowboys.
   Ⓒ life in the Old West.
   Ⓓ what cowboys wear.

2. Which words belong in Box 1?
   Ⓐ were lazy
   Ⓑ were very old
   Ⓒ wore big hats
   Ⓓ wore fancy suits

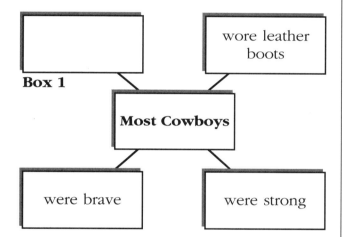

Box 1

wore leather boots

Most Cowboys

were brave

were strong

3. Which statement is *not* true?
   Ⓐ Cowboys sometimes have to work in the cold and the rain.
   Ⓑ Cowboys often work from early morning to night.
   Ⓒ Cowboys never have to drive cattle across great distances.
   Ⓓ Cowboys use a rope to catch and tie cattle.

4. The word *vaqueros* comes from the Spanish word *vaca,* which means
   Ⓐ rope.
   Ⓑ shade.
   Ⓒ hero.
   Ⓓ cow.

5. The main job of the *vaqueros* was to
   Ⓐ take care of cattle.
   Ⓑ build huge ranches.
   Ⓒ act in movies.
   Ⓓ plant crops.

Answers

1. Ⓐ Ⓑ Ⓒ Ⓓ
2. Ⓐ Ⓑ Ⓒ Ⓓ
3. Ⓐ Ⓑ Ⓒ Ⓓ
4. Ⓐ Ⓑ Ⓒ Ⓓ
5. Ⓐ Ⓑ Ⓒ Ⓓ

Go on ➤

6. The article points out that the first cowboys were
   Ⓐ Spanish settlers.
   Ⓑ Mexican Indians.
   Ⓒ from California and Utah.
   Ⓓ from Nevada.

7. The writer suggests that today's cowboys
   Ⓐ do not have many skills.
   Ⓑ live mainly in the East.
   Ⓒ owe much to the *vaqueros* of long ago.
   Ⓓ are no longer called buckaroos.

8. The territory later became California and Nevada. The word *territory* means
   Ⓐ land.
   Ⓑ lakes.
   Ⓒ streets.
   Ⓓ towns.

9. Many Americans admire people who work hard and are independent. When you are *independent,* you
   Ⓐ are not sure of what to do.
   Ⓑ always do what other people tell you to do.
   Ⓒ keep asking others for help.
   Ⓓ think and act on your own.

10. Some of today's cowboys are the descendants of the Mexican *vaqueros.* What are *descendants?*
    Ⓐ people who are born to a family or group
    Ⓑ good friends
    Ⓒ teachers
    Ⓓ neighbors

Answers

6.	Ⓐ	Ⓑ	Ⓒ	Ⓓ
7.	Ⓐ	Ⓑ	Ⓒ	Ⓓ
8.	Ⓐ	Ⓑ	Ⓒ	Ⓓ
9.	Ⓐ	Ⓑ	Ⓒ	Ⓓ
10.	Ⓐ	Ⓑ	Ⓒ	Ⓓ

How many questions did you answer correctly? Circle your score below. Then fill in your **Comprehension** score on the **Test-Taker Score Chart** on the inside of the back cover.

Number Correct	1	2	3	4	5	6	7	8	9	10
My Score	10	20	30	40	50	60	70	80	90	100

Go on ➤

II. Mechanics (capitalization, punctuation, the comma, spelling, and grammar)

Fill in the circle next to the correct answer.

1. Which sentence has a mistake in capitalization?
   - Ⓐ California, Nevada, and Utah are some western states.
   - Ⓑ Years ago, spanish settlers built huge ranches in Mexico.
   - Ⓒ They taught the Americans how to rope cattle.
   - Ⓓ They brought animals never before seen in North America.

2. Which sentence has a mistake in punctuation?
   - Ⓐ Dr Luis Ramirez has written a book about cowboys.
   - Ⓑ Have you read that book?
   - Ⓒ It's easy to recognize cowboys by the clothes they wear.
   - Ⓓ They must have strength, courage, and endurance.

3. Which sentence needs a comma or does not use the comma correctly?
   - Ⓐ The *vaqueros,* the first cowboys, lived in small huts.
   - Ⓑ They used ropes for catching and tying up cattle.
   - Ⓒ Did you learn a lot about the early cowboys Emily?
   - Ⓓ Yes, I learned a lot about the early cowboys.

4. Which sentence has a mistake in spelling in the **underlined** word?
   - Ⓐ Some *vaqueros* could rope a <u>running</u> animal.
   - Ⓑ The early settlers kept <u>there</u> cattle on ranches.
   - Ⓒ The article tells about things that <u>happened</u> many years ago.
   - Ⓓ They led very <u>busy</u> lives.

5. Which sentence has a mistake in grammar?
   - Ⓐ Many movies show cowboys as heroes.
   - Ⓑ The *vaqueros* rode horses very well.
   - Ⓒ They drove cattle across great distances.
   - Ⓓ Many English words comes from Spanish words.

Answers

1. Ⓐ Ⓑ Ⓒ Ⓓ
2. Ⓐ Ⓑ Ⓒ Ⓓ
3. Ⓐ Ⓑ Ⓒ Ⓓ
4. Ⓐ Ⓑ Ⓒ Ⓓ
5. Ⓐ Ⓑ Ⓒ Ⓓ

How many questions did you answer correctly? Circle your score below. Then fill in your **Mechanics** score on the **Test-Taker Score Chart** on the inside of the back cover.

Number Correct	1	2	3	4	5
Your Score	20	40	60	80	100

Go on ➤

III. Writing

Answer the questions. You may look back at the article as often as you wish.

1. Read this sentence from the article.

   A *vaquero* lived a very hard life.

   Use facts and examples from the article to show that this statement is true.

   _____

   _____

   _____

   _____

   _____

   _____

2. What were some of the things that the *vaqueros* taught the new American cowboys? Fill in the chart below.

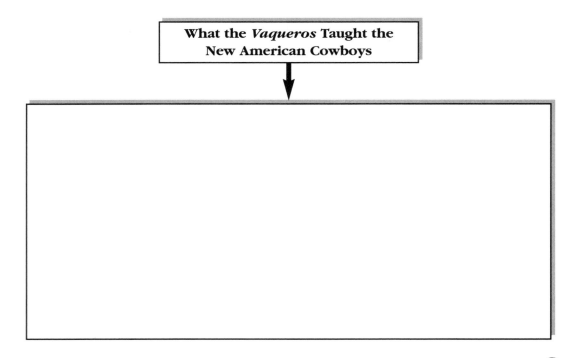

What the *Vaqueros* Taught the New American Cowboys

Go on ➤

3. Skim the article. Find three English words that come from Spanish words. Then fill in the chart.

English Word	What Word Means in English	Spanish Word	What Word Means in Spanish

4. Do you think you would have liked living in the Old West? Give some reasons to support your answer.

_____

_____

_____

_____

_____

_____

_____

_____

_____

DIRECTIONS
Read the story below. Then answer the questions
that follow.

A Guest for the Night

You may think you
have heard
everything. But
you probably
haven't heard about
Primo Antonio and the
night that his coach
broke down. Although some
people claim that the story
never happened, I think it is true.
You can decide for yourself.

The year was 1872. The great opera
singer Primo Antonio was traveling by horse
and coach. He had sung in all the great opera houses in
Europe. Now he was on his way to El Paso, Texas, to sing in
the new opera house there. He had just sung in Laredo and the
crowds had loved him. They cheered and cheered, threw roses
onto the stage, and kept calling out his name.

"I am so lucky," Primo Antonio was thinking. "I can't
imagine anyone luckier than I am."

You can probably guess what happened next. Just as he
was thinking about his good luck—*bang*! One of the wheels on
the coach suddenly fell off.

Antonio inspected the damage and realized that he could go
no farther. It was getting dark and he was tired, so he tied up
his horses and went to find help.

Soon he came to a house where a light was burning. He
knocked on the door, and a moment later a man stood before
him.

For additional exercises and another story about a guest, see "A Guest for Halil"
in *More Surprises* in *Goodman's Five-Star Stories,* Level D.

"Excuse me for bothering you at such a late hour," said Primo Antonio, "but I am afraid I need some assistance. My coach has broken down. I wonder if you could direct me to a nearby hotel where I can spend the night."

The man stared at him for a long time. At first Antonio thought that he was angry. But then the man cried out, "Why, you are Primo Antonio!"

"Well, yes, I am," Antonio admitted.

"I just saw you in Laredo!" the man exclaimed. "You were great! You gave the most wonderful performance I have ever seen in my life!"

"Thank you very much," said Antonio. "That is nice of you to say. But can you tell me where I can find a hotel?"

"A hotel! I would never dream of sending the great Primo Antonio to a hotel! No, you will stay here as my guest. My name is James Wilson, and you will eat and drink and sleep in my house! It may not be like the great houses of Europe, but I think you will find it very comfortable. Please, Mr. Antonio, I will not take no for an answer!"

How could Antonio refuse? He agreed to stay for the night.

Before long he was glad he had done so, for James Wilson prepared a delicious meal. Later, Antonio was led to a private bathroom. There he bathed with fine soap and dried himself with soft towels. That night he slept on silk sheets and goose feather pillows. The next morning he was given a very big breakfast.

"This has all been wonderful," said Antonio. "How can I ever pay you back?"

"That's easy," said James Wilson. "Here is the bill."

Wilson handed Antonio a piece of paper on which was written:

1 dinner	$2.50
soap	$.30
hot water	$.10
1 towel	$.25
overnight stay (man)	$3.00
overnight stay (horses)	$2.00
1 breakfast	$1.25
Total	$9.40

"You can pay me in cash or in gold," said James Wilson.

"What!" cried Primo Antonio. "You are giving me a bill! You expect me to *pay* you?"

"Well," said Wilson, "didn't you stay here? Didn't you eat my food and sleep in my house? Didn't I take care of your horses for you?"

"Of course, but you said I would be your *guest*."

"I'll tell you what," said Wilson. "Let's go to the town judge and tell him the story. Do you agree to accept what he says?"

"Yes!" said Antonio. "Just wait until he hears this. He'll probably have you locked up."

The two men went to see the judge at the courthouse.

"What seems to be the trouble?" the judge asked.

With great relief, Antonio told the judge the whole story.

"I see," said the judge. He returned to Wilson. "And you, sir." he said. "What is *your* side of the story?"

"I have no side," said Wilson. "Everything he said is perfectly true."

"Well then," said the judge, "let me think this over."

He was silent for a few seconds. Then he said, "Gentlemen, I have given this matter great thought, and here is what I have decided. Mr. Antonio must pay the bill."

Primo Antonio was amazed. He could not believe what he heard. But what could he do? The judge had ruled.

The two men left the building. Antonio took out his wallet and started to count out some bills.

"Mr. Antonio, what are you doing?" asked Wilson.

"Why, I'm paying you the money I owe you."

"Owe me? You owe me nothing! You were my guest! It was my pleasure to serve the great Primo Antonio."

"But . . . but what about the bill? What about making me come here?"

"Oh, *that*," smiled James Wilson. "Don't worry about *that*. I just wanted you to see what a fool we have for a judge in this town."

Go on ➤

I. Reading Comprehension Skills

Fill in the circle next to the correct answer.

1. This story is mostly about
   Ⓐ what happens when an opera singer gets a bill that he does not expect.
   Ⓑ the problems that singers must face.
   Ⓒ how hard it is to be a judge.
   Ⓓ why you should never travel alone.

2. Primo Antonio had to find help when
   Ⓐ he became sick.
   Ⓑ he fell off his coach.
   Ⓒ his horses ran away.
   Ⓓ a wheel fell off his coach.

3. James Wilson told the judge that
   Ⓐ Antonio was not telling the truth.
   Ⓑ everything that Antonio said was true.
   Ⓒ he was very angry because Antonio refused to pay the bill.
   Ⓓ he was willing to charge Antonio less for the night's stay.

4. Which statement is true?
   Ⓐ Primo Antonio had never been to Europe.
   Ⓑ James Wilson received $9.20 from Primo Antonio.
   Ⓒ Wilson never intended to take any money from Antonio.
   Ⓓ The judge said that James Wilson was wrong.

5. Which statement is *not* true?
   Ⓐ Antonio ate dinner and breakfast at James Wilson's house.
   Ⓑ Antonio bathed with fine soap.
   Ⓒ Antonio was given a fine silk suit.
   Ⓓ Antonio slept on a bed that had goose feather pillows.

6. We may infer (figure out) that James Wilson
   Ⓐ wanted to make money by charging for the use of his house.
   Ⓑ tried to force Primo Antonio to sing for him.
   Ⓒ did not really like opera.
   Ⓓ was sure that the judge would make a foolish choice.

Answers			
1. Ⓐ	Ⓑ	Ⓒ	Ⓓ
2. Ⓐ	Ⓑ	Ⓒ	Ⓓ
3. Ⓐ	Ⓑ	Ⓒ	Ⓓ
4. Ⓐ	Ⓑ	Ⓒ	Ⓓ
5. Ⓐ	Ⓑ	Ⓒ	Ⓓ
6. Ⓐ	Ⓑ	Ⓒ	Ⓓ

Go on ➤

7. The main purpose of the story is to
   (A) amuse the reader.
   (B) teach an important lesson.
   (C) scare the reader.
   (D) make the reader feel sad.

8. He inspected the damage to the coach. The word *inspected* means
   (A) caused.
   (B) did not care about.
   (C) looked at carefully.
   (D) forgot about.

9. Primo Antonio said that he needed assistance. The word *assistance* means
   (A) friends.
   (B) food.
   (C) shelter.
   (D) help.

10. Antonio gave a wonderful performance. A *performance* is a
    (A) show.
    (B) trip.
    (C) meal.
    (D) promise.

Answers

7.	Ⓐ	Ⓑ	Ⓒ	Ⓓ
8.	Ⓐ	Ⓑ	Ⓒ	Ⓓ
9.	Ⓐ	Ⓑ	Ⓒ	Ⓓ
10.	Ⓐ	Ⓑ	Ⓒ	Ⓓ

How many questions did you answer correctly? Circle your score below. Then fill in your **Comprehension** score on the **Test-Taker Score Chart** on the inside of the back cover.

Number Correct	1	2	3	4	5	6	7	8	9	10
My Score	10	20	30	40	50	60	70	80	90	100

Go on ▶

II. Mechanics (capitalization, punctuation, the comma, spelling, and grammar)

Fill in the circle next to the correct answer.

1. Which sentence has a mistake in capitalization?
   - Ⓐ Primo Antonio had sung in many opera houses in Europe.
   - Ⓑ He stayed at the home of Mr. James Wilson.
   - Ⓒ The judge asked, "what is your side of the story?"
   - Ⓓ He said, "You are the best singer I have ever heard in my life."

2. Which sentence has a mistake in punctuation?
   - Ⓐ Primo Antonio was on his way to El Paso Texas.
   - Ⓑ Wilson charged Antonio for breakfast, dinner, soap, and hot water.
   - Ⓒ Antonio couldn't believe what the judge decided.
   - Ⓓ Do you think that this story is true?

3. Which sentence needs commas or does not use the comma correctly?
   - Ⓐ No, I do not think that this story is true.
   - Ⓑ He lost a wheel on his coach, and his horses were tired.
   - Ⓒ The crowd cheered and called out his name.
   - Ⓓ Primo Antonio a great opera singer was traveling by coach.

4. Which sentence has a mistake in spelling in the **underlined** word?
   - Ⓐ Antonio was willing to <u>accept</u> what the judge said.
   - Ⓑ However, he was <u>suprised</u> by what the judge said.
   - Ⓒ Antonio <u>believed</u> he did not have to pay the bill.
   - Ⓓ At the <u>beginning</u> of the story, Antonio's coach broke down.

5. Which sentence has a mistake in grammar?
   - Ⓐ Primo Antonio and James Wilson is two characters in the story.
   - Ⓑ Antonio spent a night at the home of James Wilson.
   - Ⓒ Both men went to see the judge.
   - Ⓓ The judge did his best.

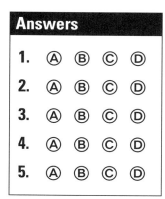

Answers

1. Ⓐ Ⓑ Ⓒ Ⓓ
2. Ⓐ Ⓑ Ⓒ Ⓓ
3. Ⓐ Ⓑ Ⓒ Ⓓ
4. Ⓐ Ⓑ Ⓒ Ⓓ
5. Ⓐ Ⓑ Ⓒ Ⓓ

How many questions did you answer correctly? Circle your score below. Then fill in your **Mechanics** score on the **Test-Taker Score Chart** on the inside of the back cover.

Number Correct	1	2	3	4	5
Your Score	20	40	60	80	100

Go on ➤

III. Writing

Answer the questions. You may look back at the story as
often as you wish.

1. Below are some events that took place in "A Guest for the
   Night." Use the chart to put the events in the order in
   which they happened. Write the correct letter in each box.
   The first letter has been done for you.

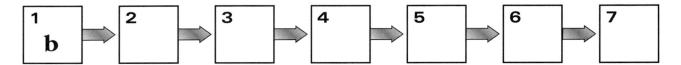

   a. Later, James Wilson gave Primo Antonio a bill.

   b. Primo Antonio's coach broke down.

   c. James Wilson insisted that Antonio stay as his guest.

   d. Wilson said that Antonio did not owe him anything.

   e. Wilson gave Antonio a delicious dinner and a big breakfast.

   f. They told the story to a judge.

   g. The judge ruled that Antonio had to pay the bill.

2. Now use the events in the chart to tell what happened in
   the story. Put the events in the correct order.

_____

_____

_____

_____

_____

_____

_____

_____

_____

Go on ➤

3. Suppose that James Wilson had been the one to tell the story to the judge. What do you think Wilson might have told the judge? Write Wilson's words below.

You see it was this way, judge. It all started when _____

_____

_____

_____

_____

_____

_____

_____

_____

4. James Wilson thought that the judge was a fool. Do you agree with him? Explain your answer.

_____

_____

_____

_____

_____

_____

_____

_____

Stop

One Thousand Paper Cranes

The story of Sadako Sasaki has touched people all over the world. Sadako was only two years old when the atomic bomb was dropped on Hiroshima at the end of World War II. She was living in Hiroshima with her family when the bomb exploded on August 6, 1945.

At the time, it did not seem that the bomb hurt Sadako, and everyone expected her to grow up strong and healthy. But 10 years later, in 1955, something terrible began to happen. Sadako started to feel sick. She was dizzy and felt tired all the time.

Sadako's parents took her to the hospital where the doctors told them the sad news. Sadako was very sick. The sickness was caused by radiation—a kind of poison that was released when the bomb exploded. The doctors were afraid that Sadako might die.

Sadako stayed in the hospital and tried to get better. She kept hoping that one day she would recover and would be able to go back to school and see her friends. Sadako was on her school's track team. More than anything else, she wanted to be healthy and to be able to run.

For additional exercises and a theme-related story set in Japan, see "The Crane Maiden" in *More Surprises* in *Goodman's Five-Star Stories,* Level D.

One day Sadako's best friend, Chizuko, came to visit Sadako in the hospital. Chizuko stood by Sadako's bedside and told her to close her eyes. When Sadako opened them again, Chizuko was holding a pair of scissors and a piece of gold paper.

"What are you doing with that?" asked Sadako.

"I know how you can get better," replied Chizuko. "Watch!" Chizuko cut the gold paper into a square. Then she began folding the square again and again. Before long, she showed the paper to Sadako. It had been folded to look like a beautiful crane.

"But how can this crane make me better?" asked Sadako.

Chizuko answered, "Long ago, people believed that cranes lived for a thousand years. There is an old story about the crane. The story says that if a sick person makes a thousand paper cranes, the gods may make that person healthy again."

When Sadako heard this, she began to cry. Oh, how she wanted to get better! She closed her eyes and wished for good health.

Chizuko showed Sadako how to fold paper into the shape of a crane. Very soon Sadako had folded 10 paper cranes. She felt very happy. She thought, "Now I have only nine hundred and ninety left to make. Soon I will be healthy again."

That evening Sadako's older brother, Masahiro, came to visit her. She showed him the cranes she had made, and he helped her hang them from the ceiling on thread. He promised to hang every crane that Sadako made, and she felt more hopeful than ever.

In the following days, Sadako made hundreds of cranes. Some were gold like the first one. Others were made with different colors. Soon Sadako's hospital room was filled with hanging cranes. They looked as if they were flying all around the room.

Unfortunately, Sadako did not start to feel better. In fact, she began to feel worse. She had terrible headaches and became even more tired. It became harder and harder for Sadako to make the cranes, but still she kept going. She reached 300 . . . 400. She kept on making cranes. She wanted to reach 1,000.

Finally Sadako was almost too sick to work, but she refused to stop. From her hospital bed, she made crane number 644. Then she felt too tired to make another and fell asleep. It was the last crane Sadako ever made.

Sadako Sasaki died on October 25, 1955. After she died, her classmates made another 356 cranes so that 1,000 paper cranes could be buried with Sadako. But her classmates wanted to do even more to remember her. They collected money to build a Peace Park in honor of Sadako and all the children killed by the atomic bomb. In the Peace Park in Hiroshima, Japan, there is a stone statue of Sadako holding a crane in her hands.

You can read all about Sadako Sasaki in the book *Sadako and the Thousand Paper Cranes* by Eleanor Coerr. The book concludes with the words that are on the base of Sadako's statue. These words were written by Sadako's friends. It is their wish:

"This is our cry,
This is our prayer;
Peace in the world."

Go on ➤

I. Reading Comprehension Skills

Fill in the circle next to the correct answer.

1. What is this article mostly about?
   - Ⓐ how to make paper cranes
   - Ⓑ how a girl fought to live and how she was honored
   - Ⓒ what life is like in a hospital
   - Ⓓ a Peace Park in Hiroshima

2. When did Sadako begin to feel sick?
   - Ⓐ when the atomic bomb was dropped
   - Ⓑ when she was two years old
   - Ⓒ five years after the bomb was dropped
   - Ⓓ in 1955, when she was 12

3. Which words belong in Box l?
   - Ⓐ showed courage
   - Ⓑ had no friends
   - Ⓒ died when she was 20
   - Ⓓ never got tired

4. Why did Sadako fold paper cranes?
   - Ⓐ She had nothing better to do.
   - Ⓑ She hoped that would help her to get well.
   - Ⓒ She liked to make paper animals.
   - Ⓓ The doctors asked her to do that.

5. Sadako had terrible headaches and was very ill, but she
   - Ⓐ kept going to school.
   - Ⓑ finally got well.
   - Ⓒ refused to stop making paper cranes.
   - Ⓓ spent a few days at home each week.

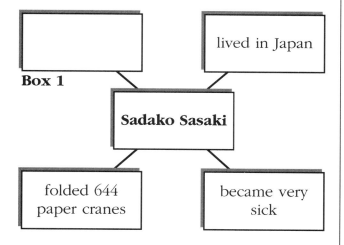

Box 1

lived in Japan

Sadako Sasaki

folded 644 paper cranes

became very sick

Answers

1. Ⓐ Ⓑ Ⓒ Ⓓ
2. Ⓐ Ⓑ Ⓒ Ⓓ
3. Ⓐ Ⓑ Ⓒ Ⓓ
4. Ⓐ Ⓑ Ⓒ Ⓓ
5. Ⓐ Ⓑ Ⓒ Ⓓ

Go on ➤

6. Which sentence is true?

    Ⓐ Sadako was buried with 1,000 paper cranes.

    Ⓑ In the Peace Park there is a statue of Sadako holding a book.

    Ⓒ The cranes that Sadako folded were all the same color.

    Ⓓ Sadako's brother, Masahiro, did not help her.

7. The story ends with a wish for

    Ⓐ more doctors to help people who are sick.

    Ⓑ good health to everyone.

    Ⓒ better hospitals.

    Ⓓ peace in the world.

8. A kind of poison was released when the bomb exploded. The word *released* means

    Ⓐ let go.

    Ⓑ kept in.

    Ⓒ tasted.

    Ⓓ found.

9. Sadako hoped that one day she would finally recover. As used here, the word *recover* means

    Ⓐ to stand up.

    Ⓑ to walk around.

    Ⓒ to get well.

    Ⓓ to play games.

10. Eleanor Coerr's book about Sadako concludes with words written by Sadako's friends. The word *concludes* means

    Ⓐ asks.

    Ⓑ needs.

    Ⓒ helps.

    Ⓓ ends.

Answers

6.	Ⓐ	Ⓑ	Ⓒ	Ⓓ
7.	Ⓐ	Ⓑ	Ⓒ	Ⓓ
8.	Ⓐ	Ⓑ	Ⓒ	Ⓓ
9.	Ⓐ	Ⓑ	Ⓒ	Ⓓ
10.	Ⓐ	Ⓑ	Ⓒ	Ⓓ

How many questions did you answer correctly? Circle your score below. Then fill in your **Comprehension** score on the **Test-Taker Score Chart** on the inside of the back cover.

Number Correct	1	2	3	4	5	6	7	8	9	10
My Score	10	20	30	40	50	60	70	80	90	100

Go on ➤

II. Mechanics (capitalization, punctuation, the comma, spelling, and grammar)

Fill in the circle next to the correct answer.

1. Which sentence has a mistake in capitalization?
   - Ⓐ Sadako Sasaki was living in Japan when the atomic bomb exploded.
   - Ⓑ It exploded on august 6, 1945.
   - Ⓒ There is a statue of Sadako in the Peace Park in Hiroshima.
   - Ⓓ You can read more about Sadako in a book by Eleanor Coerr.

2. Which sentence is not punctuated correctly?
   - Ⓐ Mr and Mrs Sasaki took Sadako to the hospital.
   - Ⓑ Sadako's brother visited her at the hospital.
   - Ⓒ Oh, how she wanted to get better!
   - Ⓓ Sadako's classmates didn't forget her.

3. Which sentence needs a comma or does not use the comma correctly?
   - Ⓐ Sadako's best friend, Chizuko, told her the story of the cranes.
   - Ⓑ Sadako stayed in the hospital and tried to get better.
   - Ⓒ It became harder for Sadako to make cranes, but she kept going.
   - Ⓓ Sadako died on October 25 1955.

4. Which sentence has a mistake in spelling in the underlined word?
   - Ⓐ Something <u>terrible</u> happened to Sadako.
   - Ⓑ She made cranes until she was <u>too</u> tired to go on.
   - Ⓒ Sadako kept <u>hopeing</u> that she would get better.
   - Ⓓ Sadako's friends wished for <u>peace</u> in the world.

5. Which sentence has a mistake in grammar?
   - Ⓐ People all over the world heard about Sadako.
   - Ⓑ The doctors were afraid that she might die.
   - Ⓒ Sadako done her best to get well.
   - Ⓓ However, she began to get sicker.

Answers

1.	Ⓐ	Ⓑ	Ⓒ	Ⓓ
2.	Ⓐ	Ⓑ	Ⓒ	Ⓓ
3.	Ⓐ	Ⓑ	Ⓒ	Ⓓ
4.	Ⓐ	Ⓑ	Ⓒ	Ⓓ
5.	Ⓐ	Ⓑ	Ⓒ	Ⓓ

How many questions did you answer correctly? Circle your score below. Then fill in your **Mechanics** score on the **Test-Taker Score Chart** on the inside of the back cover.

Number Correct	1	2	3	4	5
Your Score	20	40	60	80	100

Go on ➤

III. Writing

Answer the questions. You may look back at the article as
often as you wish.

1. Read the following sentence from the article.

   The story of Sadako Sasaki has touched people all over the world.

   Explain why this is so. Use facts and examples from the
   article to support your answer.

   _____

   _____

   _____

   _____

   _____

   _____

2. What do you think must happen for there to be lasting
   peace in the world? On the chart below, list some of the
   things that you think are necessary.

Peace in the World

3. Suppose you were telling the story of Sadako Sasaki to a friend. What would you say? Write your words on the lines below.

   Be sure to check your writing for correct spelling, capitalization, punctuation, and grammar.

   _____

   _____

   _____

   _____

   _____

   _____

   _____

   _____

   _____

   _____

   _____

   _____

   _____

   _____

   _____

   _____

   _____

   _____

   _____

Go on ➤

IV. Study Skills

Reading a map. Below is part of a map of downtown Hiroshima. Use the map and the compass directions to answer the questions that follow.

Hiroshima

1. The statue of Sadako is in the Peace Park (Peace Memorial Park) in Hiroshima. Is the park in the northern, southern, eastern, or western part of downtown?

_____

2. Which structure on the map is closest to the Peace Park?

_____

Go on ➤

3. Is Hiroshima Castle in the northern or the southern part of the city?

_____

4. In what direction would you walk to get to the Shukkei-en Garden from Hiroshima Castle.

_____

5. What is the name of the river in the western part of the city?

_____

6. If you were in Hijiyama Park, would you be in the southwest or the southeast part of downtown Hiroshima?

_____

7. To get to the railroad station from the Peace Park, would you walk northeast or southwest?

_____

8. Name three other places on the map that have not yet been mentioned.

   a. _____

   b. _____

   c. _____

The Woman of His Dreams

based on a story by O. Henry

*When it comes to stories with surprise
endings, no writer is more famous than
O. Henry. All of his 300 stories end with
a surprise. See if you can guess the
surprise ending in this one.*

It was after five o'clock, and there was no one
in the office except Bill Hartley. He was only 29
years old, but Hartley was much richer than
most men his age. He liked to say, "I am not smarter
than other people, I just work harder than they do. When
I put my mind to getting something, nothing can stop me."

The silence in the office was suddenly broken by the sound
of footsteps in the hall. A man with an air of mystery about
him came in the door. The man was the detective that Hartley
had hired.

"I have found where she lives," the detective announced.
"Here is her address."

Hartley took the piece of paper that had been torn out of
the detective's notebook. On it were written the words "Vera
Arlington" and an address on East 12th Street.

The detective went on, "She moved there one week ago. If
you want me to follow her, I can—"

For additional exercises and six more stories by O. Henry that end with a surprise,
see "The Romance of the Busy Broker," "The Gift of the Magi," and "One Thousand
Dollars" in *Surprises* and "After Twenty Years," "A Service of Love," and "Mammon
and the Archer" in *More Surprises* in *Goodman's Five-Star Stories,* Level D.

"There is no need for that," Hartley interrupted. "I just wanted the address."

Hartley paid the detective and sent him on his way. Then Hartley left the office and signaled for a taxi. It took him to a distant part of the city. At one time the area had been one of the city's finest. Now it was filled with buildings that were badly in need of repair.

The taxi stopped in front of the apartment building that Hartley was seeking. The front door of the building was open, and Hartley hurried up the stairs to the second floor.

There he saw Vera standing in an open doorway. With a nod and a bright smile, she invited him inside. Vera was 21 years old, and anyone looking at her would have thought her beautiful.

"Vera," said Hartley in a voice filled with pain. "Why didn't you answer my last letter? It took me a week to discover where you had moved to. Why have you been silent when you knew how anxious I was to hear from you?"

Vera looked thoughtfully out the window. Finally she said, "I hardly know what to tell you. I understand the advantages of your offer, and sometimes I think I could be happy with you. But I am not sure. I am a city girl, and I don't know if I would like living in the country."

Hartley replied, "But haven't I told you that you can have anything you want? You can go to the city as often as you like. You can go to the theater, go shopping, see your friends. Don't you know I am a man of my word?"

Vera said, "Yes, of course. I know that you are the kindest of men. And I know that whoever you get will be very lucky." Vera sighed and looked down at her hands.

Suddenly Hartley was filled with jealousy. He said, "Tell me, Vera. Is . . . is there someone else?"

Vera paused and said, "You should not ask me that, but I will answer your question. There is another. But I have promised him nothing."

"His name!" demanded Hartley.

"Townsend."

"Raymond Townsend!" exclaimed Hartley. "How did that man come to know you? And after all I have done for him! Vera, please say that you'll come to me. You will never regret it!"

Vera looked him in the eye. Then she said very slowly, "And what about Helen?"

Hartley folded his arms and paced up and down the room. Finally he stopped and declared, "Yes, of course. You are right. I will never see her again. I will tell her tonight!"

Vera said, "Then my answer is yes. Come to me after you have spoken to Helen."

Hartley could hardly believe his good fortune. "Promise me," he said. "Give me your word."

"I promise," Vera said softly.

At the door, Hartley turned and gazed happily at Vera. "Tomorrow," he said.

"Tomorrow," she repeated.

An hour and forty minutes later, Hartley stepped off the train in the town of Floralhurst. Two minutes later he walked up the path of the wide, green lawn of his beautiful country home.

He was met at the door by a woman with long, black hair. The woman was his wife. She said, "Bill, my mother is here. She came to have dinner with us—but dinner, as usual, has been delayed."

"I have something to tell you," said Hartley. He whispered a few words into his wife's ear.

His wife cried out with joy. Her mother came running into the room.

"Oh, mother!" the dark-haired woman called out. "Guess what? Vera is coming to cook for us!"

The woman turned to her husband. "And now, Bill dear, you must go right into the kitchen and fire Helen. We have been waiting for hours, and dinner still is not ready."

Go on ➤

I. Reading Comprehension Skills

Fill in the circle next to the correct answer.

1. What is this story mostly about?
   Ⓐ what a detective does
   Ⓑ the life of a young woman
   Ⓒ places to see in the city
   Ⓓ how a man succeeds in what he sets out to do

2. Which words belong in Box 1?
   Ⓐ was not married
   Ⓑ was lazy
   Ⓒ usually got what he wanted
   Ⓓ lived in an apartment house

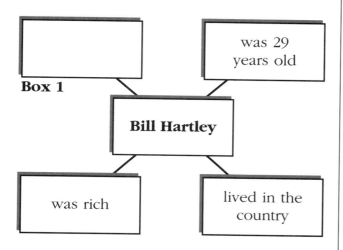

Box 1

was 29 years old

Bill Hartley

was rich

lived in the country

3. At first, the writer tries to make you think that Hartley
   Ⓐ loves Vera.
   Ⓑ does not care about Vera.
   Ⓒ has run away from Vera.
   Ⓓ is happy that Vera has gone away.

4. Which statement is true?
   Ⓐ Vera did not like Hartley.
   Ⓑ Helen often served dinner late.
   Ⓒ Vera wanted Helen to stay.
   Ⓓ The family was very happy with Helen.

5. Raymond Townsend probably asked Vera to
   Ⓐ marry him.
   Ⓑ cook for him.
   Ⓒ go shopping with him.
   Ⓓ introduce him to her friends.

Answers

1. Ⓐ Ⓑ Ⓒ Ⓓ
2. Ⓐ Ⓑ Ⓒ Ⓓ
3. Ⓐ Ⓑ Ⓒ Ⓓ
4. Ⓐ Ⓑ Ⓒ Ⓓ
5. Ⓐ Ⓑ Ⓒ Ⓓ

Go on ➤

6. At the end of the story, we discover that Vera is

Ⓐ a cook.

Ⓑ rich.

Ⓒ in love with Hartley.

Ⓓ Hartley's wife.

7. The main purpose of the story is to

Ⓐ teach the reader a lesson.

Ⓑ give the reader important information.

Ⓒ amuse the reader.

Ⓓ scare the reader.

8. Hartley found the apartment building he was seeking. The word *seeking* means

Ⓐ looking for.

Ⓑ fixing.

Ⓒ buying.

Ⓓ selling.

9. There were many advantages to accepting the offer. The word *advantages* means things that

Ⓐ can hurt you.

Ⓑ can help you.

Ⓒ cost a lot of money.

Ⓓ are unusual.

10. Hartley's wife was unhappy because dinner had been delayed. The word *delayed* means

Ⓐ lost.

Ⓑ dropped.

Ⓒ served cold.

Ⓓ put off until later.

Answers

6. Ⓐ Ⓑ Ⓒ Ⓓ

7. Ⓐ Ⓑ Ⓒ Ⓓ

8. Ⓐ Ⓑ Ⓒ Ⓓ

9. Ⓐ Ⓑ Ⓒ Ⓓ

10. Ⓐ Ⓑ Ⓒ Ⓓ

How many questions did you answer correctly? Circle your score below. Then fill in your **Comprehension** score on the **Test-Taker Score Chart** on the inside of the back cover.

Number Correct	1	2	3	4	5	6	7	8	9	10
My Score	10	20	30	40	50	60	70	80	90	100

Go on ➤

II. Mechanics (capitalization, punctuation, the comma, spelling, and grammar)

Fill in the circle next to the correct answer.

1. Which sentence has a mistake in capitalization
   - Ⓐ Vera had an apartment on East 12th Street in New York City.
   - Ⓑ The detective said, "She moved there one week ago."
   - Ⓒ Bill Hartley lived in the town of Floralhurst.
   - Ⓓ He told Vera, "You knew i was anxious to hear from you."

2. Which sentence has a mistake in punctuation?
   - Ⓐ O. Henry was born in Greensboro, North Carolina.
   - Ⓑ Did you know that his real name was William Sidney Porter?
   - Ⓒ O. Henry died on June 5, 1910.
   - Ⓓ All of O. Henrys stories end with a surprise.

3. Which sentence needs a comma or does not use the comma correctly?
   - Ⓐ His country house had a wide, green lawn.
   - Ⓑ Vera looked out the window and smiled.
   - Ⓒ After Hartley finished visiting Vera agreed to work for him.
   - Ⓓ Her hair was long, black, and shiny.

4. Which sentence has a mistake in spelling in the **underlined** word?
   - Ⓐ Vera liked to go <u>shopping</u> in the city.
   - Ⓑ Hartley <u>usualy</u> got what he wanted.
   - Ⓒ He went to the city to tell Vera that the job was <u>hers</u>.
   - Ⓓ He said, "You can visit your friends as <u>often</u> as you wish."

5. Which sentence has a mistake in grammar?
   - Ⓐ Vera and Helen was cooks.
   - Ⓑ The taxi drove to a distant part of the city.
   - Ⓒ He saw Vera standing in an open doorway.
   - Ⓓ Mrs. Hartley and her mother were waiting for dinner.

Answers

1. Ⓐ Ⓑ Ⓒ Ⓓ
2. Ⓐ Ⓑ Ⓒ Ⓓ
3. Ⓐ Ⓑ Ⓒ Ⓓ
4. Ⓐ Ⓑ Ⓒ Ⓓ
5. Ⓐ Ⓑ Ⓒ Ⓓ

How many questions did you answer correctly? Circle your score below. Then fill in your **Mechanics** score on the **Test-Taker Score Chart** on the inside of the back cover.

Number Correct	1	2	3	4	5
Your Score	20	40	60	80	100

Go on ➤

III. Writing

Answer the questions. You may look back at the story as often as you wish.

1. O. Henry is famous for writing stories that end with a surprise. What is the surprise at the end of "The Woman of His Dreams"?

   _____

   _____

   _____

   _____

   _____

2. Hartley said that he sent a letter to Vera. Pretend you are Hartley. On the lines below, write what you think he said.

   Dear Vera,

   _____

   _____

   _____

   _____

   _____

   _____

   _____

   _____

   _____

                                        Sincerely,
                                        Bill Hartley

Stop